Amazon Fi

MW00890916

Everything You Should Know About Amazon Fire Stick From Beginner To Advanced

Table of Contents

INTRODUCTION 5

CHAPTER 1: AMAZON FIRE STICK ON THE GO 8

CHAPTER 2: SETTING UP THE AMAZON FIRE STICK .14

    STEP-BY-STEP GUIDE FOR SETTING UP THE AMAZON FIRE STICK 15

CHAPTER 3: APPLICATIONS YOU CAN INSTALL ON YOUR FIRE STICK 18

    INSTALLING APPLICATIONS AND GAMES..18

    SIDELOADING APPLICATIONS 19

    DOWNLOADING AND SETTING UP APPS2FIRE................................20

    HOW TO LAUNCH YOUR APPLICATIONS ON YOUR FIRE STICK 21

    APPLICATIONS YOU CAN UPLOAD ON YOUR FIRE STICK.....................21

CHAPTER 4: MEET ALEXA, YOUR VIRTUAL PERSONAL ASSISTANT 23

    HOW ALEXA WORKS 24

    ALEXA SKILLS...25

    THE LIMITS OF ALEXA..27

CHAPTER 5: AMAZON ECHO AND THE ECHO FAMILY 28

    WHAT IS AMAZON ECHO...28

    HOW ECHO WORKS...28

    SETTING UP AMAZON ECHO 29

    THE ECHO FAMILY 30

    THE ECHO SHOW DESIGN 32

    ECHO SHOW'S VIDEO CALL AND DROP IN FEATURES 33

    WHAT ECHO SPOT CAN DO FOR YOU 35

    ECHO LOOK'S DESIGN AND FEATURES 37

    SETTING UP YOUR ECHO LOOK...38

    THE ECHO LOOK APP 39

    WHAT ECHO LOOK CAN DO FOR YOU..39

    TIPS ON USING THE ECHO LOOK APP 40

ECHO ISSUES 41

CHAPTER 6: WATCH ORIGINAL CONTENT WITH AMAZON PRIME VIDEO 43

WHAT IS AMAZON PRIME 43
AMAZON PRIME VIDEO 47
HOW TO MAXIMIZE YOUR AMAZON PRIME VIDEO VIEWING 48

CHAPTER 7: VIDEO CONTENT ON DEMAND THROUGH AMAZON VIDEO 50

THE DIFFERENCE BETWEEN AMAZON PRIME VIDEO AND AMAZON VIDEO 50
1-CLICK ORDERING AND PAYMENT 51
HOW TO RENT OR BUY A VIDEO TITLE 51
WATCHING FIRST EPISODES FOR FREE 52

CHAPTER 8: CURATE YOUR OWN NICHE VIDEO CONTENT IN AMAZON CHANNELS 53

WHAT IS AMAZON CHANNELS? 53
DIFFERENCE OF AMAZON CHANNELS FROM PRIME VIDEO AND AMAZON VIDEO 55
WATCH AMAZON CHANNELS 56
WATCH LIVE VIDEO THROUGH AMAZON CHANNELS 56
DIFFERENCE OF AMAZON CHANNELS FROM NETFLIX AND HULU 57

CHAPTER 9: ENJOY UNLIMITED PHOTO AND PERSONAL VIDEO STORAGE AND SHARING 58

WHAT IS PRIME PHOTO? 58
WHAT PRIME PHOTO CAN DO FOR YOU 58
HOW TO BACK UP PHOTOS WITH YOUR PRIME PHOTO 59
MORE FEATURES FOR THE PRIME PHOTOS 62

CHAPTER 10: PRIME MUSIC AND AMAZON UNLIMITED MUSIC 63

WHAT IS AMAZON PRIME MUSIC? 63
HOW TO LOCATE YOUR PRIME MUSIC 65
DOWNLOADING PRIME MUSIC FOR OFFLINE PLAYBACK 67

WHAT IS AMAZON MUSIC UNLIMITED? 67

SUBSCRIPTION PLANS FOR MUSIC UNLIMITED 69

CHAPTER 11: TWITCH PRIME FOR GAMERS 70

WHAT IS TWITCH PRIME 70

WHAT YOU GAIN FROM TWITCH PRIME MEMBERSHIP 71

SUBSCRIBING TO TWITCH PRIME 71

CHAPTER 12: HAVE FAMILY FUN SHARING PRIME CONTENTS WITH AMAZON HOUSEHOLD 74

WHAT IS AMAZON HOUSEHOLD? 74

CREATING A HOUSEHOLD 75

SHARING FAMILY LIBRARY CONTENT 77

PIN FOR SECURE PURCHASES AND VIEWING CONTROL ...79

SHARING PRIME BENEFITS WITH THE AMAZON HOUSEHOLD 79

CONCLUSION 81

Introduction

The Amazon fire stick is one of the latest electronics streaming devices. From the time it was launched in 2014, it now evolved into its second generation with improvements and added features. It may be one of many similar products, but what takes you to the next level of entertainment experience are the new features, services and easy access to a host of movies, TV shows, music, and many more.

The *Amazon fire stick's attraction* lies in its apps which expand its contents and boost the stick's capacity to provide a variety of functionalities. The fire stick, with its wireless portability, is not only your entertainment companion, but an e-commerce personal assistant that makes e-shopping effortless and convenient. You can do almost anything you want anywhere you are at any time you want.

With the fire stick, you can:

- Watch movies which you can access from Amazon's library through the Amazon Prime, or from other third-party providers like Netflix
- Use voice search on TV with Alexa voice control
- Digital signage on your TV
- Share photos on your TV screen
- Connect to games on TV
- Listen to music
- Connect to YouTube
- Play games on TV

All these functions are given to you through the varied services contained in the Amazon Fire Stick. The streaming services offered through the Fire Stick enables the upload of various entertainment, information, and e-commerce applications and extra features, such as:

- **Alexa** – the voice-control system which gives you your virtual personal assistant
- **Amazon Echo** – the sensitive speaker companion of Alexa that makes it possible for you to interact with Alexa hands-free.
- **The Echo Family** – which broadens your Echo experience and brings it to greater heights with its specific functionalities, and for which you will be grateful for its practical use:

    o The Echo Dot
    o Echo Show
    o Echo Plus
    o Echo Spot
    o Echo Look
    o Amazon Tap

- **Amazon Video, Amazon Prime Video, and Amazon Channels** - streaming services with distinct functions catering to the different preferences of users
- **Amazon Household and sharing** capabilities which gives the family members the opportunity to experience the Amazon Fire Stick's contents and benefits together
- **Prime Photos and Personal Videos** – fun and memories which you can share and store in an unlimited storage capacity provided by your Amazon Fire Stick
- **Prime Music** – an extra feature offered by the Amazon Fire Stick which gives you ads-free access to millions of songs organized under the Prime Playlists and customized Prime Stations with no extra expense
- **Twitch Prime** – the latest gaming service of Amazon for avid gamers with extra gaming benefits.

The Amazon Fire Stick is a repository of all your favorite contents. It serves as a portal to a host of Amazon products and services, so much so that you don't have to leave your house for your needs. As a portal, the fire stick guides you to where you want to go or what you want to do to satisfy your specific requirements.

You will find the Fire Stick more enjoyable with the Alexa voice control, which is able to follow your commands by speaking to its companion Echo, the smart speaker.

This book also explains the different functionalities of applications you can download, the extra features offered by the Amazon Fire Stick, how to set up Fire Stick and its different applications, and how to make use of these apps.

It is hoped that the book will give you a comprehensive understanding of the Amazon Fire Stick so you can maximize your Fire Stick experience.

Let's begin the journey.

Chapter 1: Amazon Fire Stick On the Go

The Amazon fire stick is a streaming device for movies, TV shows, subscription services, photos, music, videos, applications, and games. You might say that there are other streaming devices to choose from in the streaming industry, foremost of which are the Google Chromecast and Roku stick.

All three are streaming devices, but what matters most to users are the services and applications that come with the hardware, and the ease with which these contents are delivered so users can make maximum use of these contents.

With Amazon's long-standing relationship with its consumers, giving this e-commerce giant the edge in knowing consumer wants and behaviors, Amazon is in the forefront of developing a technology which enables a seamless process of watching TV to buying items online through TV.

The resulting creation is the new Amazon Fire Stick, a diminutive of the Fire TV which contains similar features, though in a slightly lesser degree. The Fire TV has more features than the Amazon Fire Stick, but what matters is the fire stick's portability and specific function.

The Amazon fire stick was first introduced in 2014 to compete with Roku and Google Chromecast. The second generation Amazon Fire Stick, along with Alexa Voice Remote, was introduced in October 2016.

This new fire stick is an improved version of the first generation, which includes updates on Quad-core ARM 1.3 GHz processor with support for 32-bit apps, Mediatek 8127D system, Mali-450 MP4 GPU. The wireless hardware includes upgrades on two-band frequencies, dual-antenna which supports 2x2 MIMO 802.11a/b/g/n/ac, and a Bluetooth 4.1.

With the upgrades on the new Amazon Fire Stick, you get faster speed in streaming. By plugging the fire stick into an HDMI TV, you transform an ordinary TV into a smart TV. The size of the fire stick is about 3", which makes the device portable and ideal if you are the type of person who travels much or who would like to have your TV content handy wherever you are. Installing the stick is simple and easy to follow.

New features of the new Amazon fire stick

- A voice control system called Alexa, with a sensitive and intuitive voice recognition capacity. This feature is integrated into the Alexa voice remote which you activate by pressing down on the microphone button. The difference with the previous version of the Alexa voice control is in the commands. In the new version, in place of the standard Alexa commands, you talk into the speaker using phrases that mean the same thing, like fast forward or skip ahead and Alexa gives the same result. Another feature of the new Alexa is its ability to do a voice search for films, genres, and playback.

- An upgraded processor allows for fast flicking through menus, reducing or eliminating the waiting time for loading the pages.

- Fast streaming with the ability to learn your viewing habits through its Advanced Streaming and Prediction (ASAP). This feature pre-buffers shows what the device thinks is the subsequent show you are most likely to watch.

- In addition to Amazon's streaming apps, the fire stick now includes third-party channels, expanding the apps it accommodates, like Netflix for one, and adding to the inventory of movies you can watch. This inclusive approach extends to other apps like gaming and other services.

- The navigation menu now is on top of the screen instead of at the side, with videos and moving images that catch your attention. The new feature also learns your content preferences and adapts your preferred content.

Things to remember before buying a fire stick

The new Amazon fire stick appeals to consumers because of the added features, low price, developed by a reputable company, good reviews, upgraded hardware to accommodate all your favorite contents, and a service that boasts of top players in the streaming space.

If you plan to purchase a fire stick, it helps to be familiar with some grey areas which make most fire stick users uncertain about the purchase.

If this is your first attempt to use a streaming device, or perhaps you hesitate to get one due to some uncertainties in functionality and capability of the device, becoming knowledgeable of some significant points about the Amazon Fire Stick will help remove these doubts.

- The Fire TV stick and the Fire TV are different products.

  The Fire TV and the Fire TV stick can be confusing for the uninitiated in streaming devices or by the use of the terms. Fire is a brand name Amazon uses to identify its many products, the use of which tends to confuse consumers.

  The fire stick is a diminutive streaming device of the Fire TV. Its size is 3.4" x ½" x 0.5" compared to Fire TV's 2.6" x 2.6" x 0.6". To give you an idea of the fire TV stick's size, this device is similar to your regular flash drive.

  As a little brother to the Fire TV, the Amazon fire stick does the same thing the Fire TV does. The Fire TV, though, has more features than the fire stick and costs more.

- You need an internet connection to stream videos.

One of the more intensive streaming activities you can do on a device which is internet-connected is video streaming. The speed of streaming would depend on your internet connection speed. If your TV does not meet the required internet speed, this will slow down your streaming activity.

Netflix, a third-party service of Amazon Fire Stick, gives the following recommendations:

  - 0.5 Megabits per second – required broadband connection
  - 1.5 Megabits per second – recommended broadband connection speed
  - 3.0 Megabits per second – recommended for SD quality
  - 5.0 Megabits per second – recommended for HD quality
  - 25 Megabits per second – appropriate for Ultra HD quality

Check your internet connection speed to see if it matches with your intended fire stick.

- Purchase of the Amazon Fire Stick does not include Amazon Prime and Amazon Prime Video.

Amazon Prime is a membership program of Amazon which gives its members access to more services not available to ordinary fire stick users. It is a paid service that offers members advantages non-members do not enjoy. Amazon Prime also provides access to Amazon Prime Video, a streaming service which gives you access to thousands of movies at no cost.

If you purchase an Amazon fire stick, you get a free trial period for the Amazon Prime Video. You get to enjoy the services of this streaming service only for the duration of the trial period.

Further, subscription to Amazon Prime Video does not give you full access to the Amazon library. The Amazon video library includes a catalog subset which you may need to subscribe to a third-party channel, purchase, or buy.

You do not really need the Amazon Prime and the Amazon Prime Video if you are a casual gamer or movie streamer. It is better, though, to subscribe to Amazon Prime and Amazon Prime Video if you want to broaden your entertainment experience and maximize the use of your fire stick.

- You can download many streaming applications to your Amazon Fire Stick but you need paid subscriptions to use them.

The Amazon Fire Stick has a channel store which you can browse to find a streaming application and download to the device for free. Once you use the downloaded application, you will be asked to supply account information before you can use it.

The fire stick contains a file of streaming applications, but the more popular ones require paid subscriptions. Paid subscriptions would include Netflix, HBO now, Hulu and more.

- If your TV has no HDMI port, you need additional hardware and cable for the Amazon Fire Stick.

The Amazon Fire Stick supports an HDMI port, which makes connection to your TV HDMI port convenient since you won't need extra cables for connectivity. But, the stick only supports HDMI. This becomes a problem if your TV has no HDMI port.

You can solve this problem through an HDMI converter. Connect your fire stick to the HDMI converter, which is then connected to the TV with RCA cables (the tricolor of red, white and yellow).

Note that with this method of converting your TV, your video may not perform well with HD content due to the limitations of the RCA cables.

- Video streaming uses a lot of data

Video streaming uses a lot of data, a fact most users new to streaming may not know.

Data usage is not a problem if you are streaming videos via the fire stick and your home internet connection has no required maximum consumption or data caps. It is also not a problem if you don't get to pay for extra usage beyond that required of your monthly fixed payment.

Video streaming becomes an issue if you are using your fire stick with your phone. Streaming video through phones adds data quickly. The standard definition video uses 1 GB data per hour, and the high definition uses 3 GB of data per hour.

For example, if you watch a movie each night for 3 hours, in effect you used 270 GB of data for one month. The data usage, therefore, have implications to your data space on your computer and other devices, and to your finances.

Chapter 2: Setting up the Amazon Fire Stick

Setting up the Amazon Fire Stick is quite simple. But before you connect the device, check if your TV is compatible with the Amazon fire stick and if your TV has an HDMI port. The Amazon Fire Stick is compatible with high-definition and ultra-high definition TV. You would need an internet connection to open the content, such as movies, games, music, TV shows, and apps which are available free on the Amazon Fire TV. If you hold an Amazon account, register the device so you can access content and functionalities that would make the Amazon Fire TV work. If you don't have an Amazon account, you need to create one.

You can also use the Amazon fire stick on your computer monitor, provided it has an HDMI port. Note that the Amazon fire stick will not work on an output of 4K.

When you purchase an Amazon fire stick, you will find what you need for setting up the fire stick in the package:

- Amazon Fire Stick
- Alexa voice remote
- Amazon Fire TV remote (this is included if you have the Amazon fire stick first generation or the Amazon fire stick basic edition models)
- Power adapter and a USB cable
- An HDMI extender (included if you have the Amazon fire stick with a voice remote for Alexa, fire stick first generation, and fire stick basic edition models.)
- Two AAA batteries for your remote

Step-by-step guide for setting up the Amazon Fire Stick

Once you are done checking if you have what you need to set up the Amazon fire stick, setting up the device is a breeze.

Setting up the Amazon Fire Stick

- Connect the USB cord into the USB port of your fire stick.
- Plug the other end of the cord to your power adapter
- Plug this power adapter next to a power outlet
- Use the accompanying HDMI extender to plug the stick device to your TV's HDMI port. The use of the HDMI extender, which came with the purchase, makes sure your stick fits the port.
- Open your TV and choose the corresponding HDMI input channel for the port you used in your fire stick device. A Fire Stick Logo will appear on your screen.

Setting up the Alexa remote

On the back cover of the remote you will see an arrow mark. Press your thumb on the arrow mark and slide it up. Insert the two batteries at the back of the remote. You will notice that the Alexa remote is different from other remotes. In this device, both batteries face the same direction.

When the batteries are in place and you have powered up the remote, the device will automatically pair with the fire TV stick. If automatic pairing does not occur, press Home button and holds for ten seconds until it reaches the "discovery mode" and pairs with your fire stick. Be sure to have the remote within a distance of 5 meters (or nearer) from the fire stick.

When the Alexa remote is paired with the fire stick, you will see a command to start on your TV screen.

Setting up network connection

You would need an internet connection for the Amazon fire stick to function. Connecting the device to the internet completes the physical installation of your fire stick. You can connect your fire stick to either a Wi-Fi network or through a wired or Ethernet connection.

Connecting to a Wi-Fi network. On your TV menu, go to **Settings** and select **Network**. Your fire stick will automatically detect nearby networks. Choose your network and enter your password. A message will appear on your TV requesting for your confirmation.

Connecting to a wired (Ethernet) network. You need an Ethernet adapter for this type of internet connection. You may need to purchase an Ethernet adapter for fire TV stick (second generation) as this is not included in the purchase of a fire Stick.

- Connect the Ethernet adapter to your fire stick USB port
- Connect the USB power cable to the Ethernet adapter
- Connect one end of the Ethernet cable to the Ethernet adapter
- Connect the other end of the cable to a modem or router
- On the TV menu, select the option that appears on the screen
- When the set up is complete, a confirmation message will appear on your screen

Getting started with your Amazon fire stick

To connect with your wireless network, follow the instructions that appear on your TV screen. A virtual keyboard will appear on the TV screen which you use to enter your password. Enter your password for your wireless network. A confirmation message will appear. You also have the option to save your network password to Amazon.

Register your fire stick to your Amazon account. You will have to create an Amazon account if you don't have one. It is easy to create your Amazon account through the "create account" button on the TV screen and follow the instructions.

You know when you have successfully completed the setup when the "Welcome" video appears on the screen, along with tips on how to use your Amazon fire stick.

Using the Fire TV Menu

You will find the menu on top of the screen which you will need to navigate on-screen. The menu can guide you in exploring the content of your device. You have the option to use the virtual keyboard on-screen to navigate, the arrow on your remote, or the voice command on your Alexa remote.

The following labels appear on the menu:

Home – This is where you can view your content, like apps and games, contents that are recommended for you, and other contents.

Featured content – This is where you find the available new and featured titles in your fire stick. If you use your remote, short video snippets or images get displayed on the screen.

Sponsored content - displays offered digital content which includes apps, movies, and TV shows. The ad banner also displays products available for purchase through the Amazon fire stick device. Note that these displays cannot be deleted.

The menu also displays your videos, movies and TV shows, apps, and settings.

Chapter 3: Applications You Can Install on your Fire Stick

As mentioned earlier, the Amazon fire stick's focus is on featuring Amazon media products which are accessible only through membership with the Amazon Prime. Amazon, however, partnered with third-party channels which you can access through the Amazon Channels, the latest streaming service developed by Amazon.com.

The addition of a streaming service gives you three ways of streaming your Amazon content: Amazon Prime Video, Amazon Video, and the Amazon Channels. Amazon Prime gives you access to Amazon's library of original content or programming; however, you have to be a Prime member to use the Amazon Prime service. Amazon Video allows users to purchase or rent movies or shows. In Amazon Channels, you subscribe to a third-party channel to use their streaming service.

The three options do not limit your streaming preferences as you could still add more apps and view more content, other than Amazon products, through an android. The Amazon fire stick operates on androids, therefore, you can sideload any apps that support the APK (*Android Package Kit*) file format. APK is the file used to install apps, similar to EXE files on Windows.

Installing applications and games

For installing applications and games purchased from Amazon or subscribed from third party channels:

- Go to apps in your TV menu and press select
- Browse the games and applications that are available or search for a specific title using the virtual keyboard or the Alexa remote with voice control.

- Choose a game, movie, channel, or program and highlight download, then press select
- Go to the sign-in button, press select
- Your movie, game, TV show is now ready for use on your Amazon fire stick.

Sideloading applications

If you notice that your favorite application is not in the Fire stick, no need to worry. You still can add your favorite application to the Fire Stick by using its feature of sideloading.

Sideloading is basically the process of moving your favorite file or application to your android with APK files. You know when an android supports APK files when you see ".apk" at the end of the file or application.

When you enable sideloading from your Amazon fire stick, you can run:

- Any application
- A web browser
- Music, podcasts
- Ebooks
- Movies, TV shows

Preparing your Amazon Fire Stick for sideloading

- Go to **Setting** on the menu then go to **System**.
- From the **System** menu, look for the sub-menu for **Developer Options**
- Under **Developer Options**, set the **ADB Debugging** and **Apps from Unknown Source** to "On."

    The ADB Debugging option activates the ADB link and allows you to bridge your android to your fire stick.

The Apps from Unknown Source option allows you to install applications not sourced from Appstore applications.

- Go to **Back** button on the remote, then choose **Device>About>Network**. When your fire stick's IP address appears, write this down as you will need to enter the IP address later.

Tip: Noting your IP address is important. If you fail to specify your IP address and restart your fire stick you may not be successful in sideloading. IP address changes when the DHCP server assigns a new one. Further, you would need this IP address each time you load a new application to your Fire Stick.

Downloading and setting up Apps2Fire

You would need an android or a phone to install applications on your Amazon fire stick. Apps2Fire is the quickest way to upload any application from your Android or mobile devices to your Amazon Fire Stick. You can get the Apps2Fire for free from the Play Store. Download and install the Apps2Fire on your phone.

- Download and launch Apps2Fire and go to the menu.
- In the **Menu** navigate to **Setup**, enter the IP address of your Fire Stick and click **Save**. The app is now connected to your fire stick.
- Navigate to the local apps and you will find a list of applications installed on the phone. Note that you can move to your Android, not only the applications, but all the files downloaded to your Android that ends with APK

- Locate the app you are searching for, transfer it to your phone, and select the **Install** command. The app will start loading; it may, however, take a while to complete loading. Be sure to keep your mobile awake while loading. You will receive a notification once the installation is complete.

How to launch your applications on your Fire Stick

When you have installed your applications on your fire stick, you can search and launch them. Do not worry if you do not find the installed applications in the top level "Apps" of your fire stick menu.

- On the Menu, go to **Settings**, then **Applications Menu**.
- Under **Applications Menu**, go to **Manage Installed Applications** and all your installed applications appear. Browse for the application you uploaded and press **Select**
- In the sub-category of the **Application Menu,** select the **Launch Application.**

Should you decide to remove a sideloaded application, the process is easy. If you used the Apps2Fire to install the application, just press the application icon, hold, and select **Uninstall** when it appears in the dialog box.

Another option to uninstall an application is to go to the Fire Stick **Home>Apps.** Look for the application you want and highlight it. Choose **Menu** and select **Uninstall**.

Applications you can upload on your fire stick

The hardware capacity of the Amazon fire stick has limits to how much you can upload. More advanced games, therefore, may not be appropriate for the fire stick. Further, Google restrictions prevent some applications to be uploaded to the fire stick. Another limitation is that applications which operate on portrait do not work well with the fire stick.

Uploading certain applications may be a case of trial and error for you to know what works with your fire stick and what does not. Here are some applications you can install on your fires stick:

- Kodi – you can use this for media streaming
- Firefox – use this to browse on your fire stick
- Private Internet Access – for a VPN service

- IMDb – a popular site for movies
- Podcast Addicts – useful for listening to podcasts
- SyncPro for Reddit
- Outlook – for your emails and Microsoft

Chapter 4: Meet Alexa, Your Virtual Personal Assistant

When Amazon introduced Alexa in the market, it became an instant hit. The instant popularity is not surprising, considering that Alexa fits the modern lifestyle of people where ease, speed, and convenience are of prime concerns. Imagine a scenario where you don't have to lift a finger, but simply voice a command, and Alexa powers up your TV, directs you to your favorite shows and programs, do online shopping, and operate your smart home devices.

Alexa is Amazon's voice-control system which is incorporated into the Amazon Fire Stick. This device is a cloud-based intelligent personal assistant that listens to your commands through the Echo smart speakers. Alexa is probably the best feature incorporated into the streaming device. With the Amazon echo, a smart speaker, you have a winner.

Alexa responds to the "wake word" Alexa, listens to your command, and fulfills your wishes. These commands may be simple, like play your favorite music, watch a movie or dim the lights, but Alexa's response makes your life comfortable. Alexa also "wakes up" to the call of "Echo", and "computer."

With Alexa and the wireless Amazon Echo speaker, you can do a lot of things with just the sound of your voice giving the command:

- Search the web
- Watch a movie
- Play your favorite music
- Create a to-do list
- Create a shopping list and shop online
- Ask for weather reports
- Run your smart home products

Alexa's appeal to consumers is its responsiveness. The latest generation of Alexa needs no button for activation but only a trigger word to activate it. What is important is your voice and the command for what you want.

You may encounter some quirks if you miss to set Alexa properly and other compatible smart home devices. Once you get used to your Alexa, though, it becomes more natural than speaking to a phone-based voice control.

Your Amazon Fire Stick comes with an Alexa voice-control remote. So, why have the Amazon Echo? The key to having the Echo speaker is to have the Alexa platform work for you in a more convenient and easy way. With Echo, you talk and give the command directly to the speaker, freeing you from holding on to your remote or smart phone. Switching lights or pushing buttons may be simple and no bother. But, when you experience giving the commands just by speaking, with no further manual action, you will appreciate much the difference.

How Alexa works

Alexa has a natural-language processor built into the system which makes interacting with Alexa easy. It is much responsive that you don't have to give the command or ask a question twice, the device responds at the first instance. This responsiveness is due to the sensitive microphones built into the structure of Echo devices. It listens to your voice and sends your voice to the cloud for voice recognition and command analysis.

Command analysis refers to evaluating the kind of command received like if you are requesting for music, the device will search the Amazon catalog for the music. Alexa also responds to a request for music specifying an artist and Alexa plays it back to you. If you request for the day's weather report, it searches for the answer, and a female computer voice gives you the information requested.

Alexa's functionality is not limited to the entertainment media or to your shopping needs. Most Alexa users find it useful and exciting for smart home devices as well. Alexa has the ability to make your daily home tasks easier.

At the early stage of Alexa's life, the command is limited to one action. With upgrades, Alexa is now able to receive a single command for a string of actions. For example, you can give a single command to turn off the lights in one area, for instance giving the command "turn off the kitchen", and Alexa complies by turning off all lights in that area.

Alexa Skills

In Alexa's world, a skill is a program you add to Echo for a new ability. Once a skill is added to Alexa's list or skill menu, this will apply to all Alexa devices. This feature eliminates the need to add the skill to each Alexa device you may have.

Here are some of the commands you can use with your Amazon fire stick:

Basic commands

- o "Alexa, help"
- o "Alexa, let's chat" if you have a conversation
- o "Alexa, mute/unmute"
- o "Alexa, stop/pause"
- o "Alexa, change/set volume to ..." or "Alexa, turn up/down volume"

Commands for Fire TV and Amazon Fire TV Stick

- o Fire TV control – "Alexa, play (or pause, resume, stop, rewind, fast forward) on FireTV.
- o Search TV shows or movies – "Alexa, search/find [TV show title or movie title] on Fire TV"

- For opening apps – "Alexa, open/launch [name of application] on Fire TV"
- For actor's work – "Alexa, show titles with [actor's name] on Fire TV"
- Back to home – "Alexa, return to home"

Commands for Media Control

- For playing music – "Alexa, play some music"
- For playing music on other Alexa devices – "Alexa, play [artist's name or song title] in the living room" or "Alexa, play [artist's name or song title] everywhere
- For queuing music – Alexa, play music by [name of artist]"
- Play are radio station – "Alexa, play [radio station] on ..."

These are sample commands you can do with Alexa. If you want to know more Alexa commands, Amazon provided users with the Alexa Skill kit. You can expect new skills added to Alexa with each new service added.

The limits of Alexa

Your life is easier with all the things Alexa can do. In practice, though, there are some aspects that can be annoying, if you don't have the patience.

For instance, you can create a shopping list to give to Alexa. You cannot however tick off the list in one command. Alexa can understand a command for one item, like "Alexa, add bread to the shopping list," but will fail to follow a command that says "Alexa, add bread, flour, and cheese to the shopping list." Can you imagine how irritating it is to give a command for each item if you happen to have a long shopping list.

While a favorite feature of Alexa is to ask for random questions, it does not have the ability to answer all the questions you ask. Alexa is not a web browser. If your main purpose of getting Alexa is to answer questions, Google Home would be a better place.

Chapter 5: Amazon Echo and the Echo Family

What is Amazon Echo

Amazon Echo, or the more popular abbreviated name Echo, is a smart speaker developed by Amazon.com. This device connects to Alexa, a voice-controlled intelligent virtual assistant who listens to your voice through Echo and responds to the wake word "Alexa", "Echo" or "Computer". Echo, like Alexa, has the following capabilities:

- Voice interaction
- Music playback
- Create to-do lists
- Set alarms
- Play audio books
- Provide weather reports, traffic, real-time information
- Stream podcasts

How Echo works

Echo needs an internet connection for it to work. When connected to a good wireless internet connection, communication is fast due to its minimal communication round trips, geo-distributed service endpoints, and streamable responses.

Echo never stops listening to all speech, especially when in default mode. Echo is always alert to hear the wake word for it to become active. Once activated, the device records and sends the voice commands to the cloud for voice recognition and voice command analysis. The commands are received by the Alexa Voice Service which provides and sends the appropriate responses back.

Echo is equipped with seven sensitive microphones and beamforming technology which allows the device to hear you wherever you are in your home, and even when you speak low. The device is sensitive enough to hear your command even when music is playing because of its noise cancellation capability.

To set up an Echo, though, you need to have an Amazon account.

Setting up Amazon Echo

You must have an Alexa app to set up the Amazon Echo:

- Connect Echo's power supply to a wall socket
- Install Alexa app to your gadget. Alexa works well with Android, Amazon Fire phone, iOS and tablet.
- Sign in to your Amazon account. If you have no Amazon account, you need to create an account as Echo will only work if you have an active account.
- When you have completed signing in or creating an account, switch from Alexa App to your phone setting and search for the Echo in your network list.
- Tap on your Echo and it will automatically connect you since there is no need for a password.
- Go back to your Alexa App. If the app fails to start automatically, tap the three horizontal lines and go to **Settings**, then choose **Set up a New Device**. Select your home Wi-Fi network displayed on the device and enter your password.
- Your phone automatically connects to your network and announces that it is ready for use.

Note that if you have more echo devices, you need to set up the devices individually. The default wake word for Echo is Alexa, which you can change to Echo, Amazon, or Computer. You cannot, however, choose your own wake word.

If you have smart home devices, note that many of these devices require that you enable these as skills in the Alexa app. To enable the device, open the Alexa app, then choose **Menu**. In the menu, select **Skills** and search for the device's manufacturer. Some devices do not require adding it as a skill to Alexa, like Philips Hue; just press the button of Phlips Hue and ask Alexa to **Discover Devices**.

A convenient feature of Alexa is the grouping of smart home devices. You don't have to give a command for every smart home device you own, for instance, in your bedroom. You can just tell Alexa to "turn off bedroom lights" and all lights in your bedroom switches off. If you find that Alexa is not responding to your command, it might be that Alexa failed to recognize the group name. Change the group name to something that is easily understood by Alexa and speak clearly.

When starting on Echo-Alexa, you may want to go to **Things to Try** Section under the main Menu. This section introduces you to what Echo can do.

The Echo Family

Amazon has six devices offered in the market, ranging from $50 to $230, each with target functionality. With several options open to Echo users, choosing which is right for your device can be confusing.

The guide presented in this section will help you, regardless if you are new to Alexa-Echo, upgrading to a new device, or adding to your existing smart home collection.

The Echo Dot – Echo Dot is a smart speaker which serves as Amazon's portal. This speaker does the standard Echo tasks like make calls, play music, order Amazon products, and control smart home devices.

The Dot is a small 1.6 tall cylinder with a dimension of 38 x 84 x 84mm. It may be small, but it is smart. The device has no control wheel like the Amazon Echo but has four control buttons for the microphone, mute, volume up/down, and action which are positioned on top of the device.

You won't have much difficulty setting up the Dot. Once your Dot is plugged, connect to your home Wi-Fi network, download the Alexa App and Alexa will guide you step-by-step to complete the set up process.

The Dot has light indicators in different colors to indicate the device's activity:

- White moving clockwise to indicate the level of volume
- Blue and green light indicates Echo Dot is listening
- Orange appears during set up
- Red indicates a problem with the device

The Echo Dot has no speaker and needs to hook up with your existing audio set up or with Bluetooth. This device is a standalone; but, if you want to maximize Echo Dot, you can combine it with a full-size Amazon Echo. You can position the Amazon Echo in one room and the Echo Dots in your other rooms. This way, you listen to music in any room in your home.

The device is connected to always-on Alexa, which means, Echo Dot always listens to you, ready to come to life at the mention of the wake word.

The Echo Show – In this Echo family style, not only do you get an audio, but you also get a view of things on a 7-inch touch screen. With Echo Show, you see a visual display of video flash briefings, security cameras, read music lyrics, watch Amazon video, see weather forecasts, photos, to-do list, shopping list, browse audio books and listen to it; and, you do all these functions hands-free. The new most favored benefits in Echo Show are the video calling and drop in features.

Echo Show at $230 has all the features of a tablet and probably has the most functionalities of Amazon Echo, which makes the Echo show the high-end version among the Amazon Echo family.

The Echo Show is great for listening to music with its Dolby enhanced powerful speakers. The speakers produce crisp vocals and extended bass frequency response, allowing you to enjoy music to the fullest which you usually get from big monitors or big screens. With Echo Dots installed in your other rooms, you can enjoy music in any room you are in your home. The Echo Show has eight microphones with beam-forming technology which enables the device to hear you anywhere you are in the room, and even when music is playing.

The security cameras of Echo Show can show you your front door or monitor the baby. You have to install compatible cameras in places you think needs monitoring, for the security camera to function.
It is not difficult to use Echo Show. The device is designed as a voice-first device, which makes it unnecessary for additional software application and intricate interface to navigate the device.

The Echo Show Design

The Echo Show is shaped like a wedge with a choice of matte black or white outer casing. It has a dimension of 187 x 187 x 90mm, 1170g. It has a dual-band Wi-Fi connectivity which supports an 802.11 a/b/g/n (2.4 GHz, 5GHz). The accessories include a power adapter and a 6-foot cable. The security camera incorporated in the device has a 5-megapixel sensor. And, the device is connected to Alexa with its always-on, always-listening, and voice-activated features.

The 7-inch touchscreen of Echo Show has the same resolution as the Amazon Fire TV tablet which displays bright, which you can view from any angle. Controls are minimal: a blue glow at the base of the device to indicate Alexa is awake, and controls located at the top of Echo Show which allows you to change the volume, mute Alexa or stop Alexa from listening.

Echo Show's Video Call and Drop In features

The 5-megapixel camera of Echo Show allows you to make video calls, a feature which makes Echo Show attractive to Echo users. Another interesting feature, but which could also be a disturbing feature, is the Drop In feature. Note, however, that visibility could be a problem if you make night video calls as there is no light.

For video-calls to work, register your phone number to your Amazon account. Once registered, Alexa automatically scans for contacts or for other Alexa or Echo users and add these to your list of people to call or message. You will find the process seamless.

The Drop In capability allows selected contact to call and view you through Echo Show's camera at anytime. Users find this a great benefit for communicating to elderly loved ones or vice versa. There is no need to pick up your phone; you get notified by Echo Show for Drop Ins with a chime. For 10 seconds, the screen goes blurred to give you time enough to disable the camera or reject the call from unwanted video calls.

Echo Show incorporates a motion sensor which allows the device to detect when you are nearby or notify selected contacts of your approach. The device can also function as a home intercom system with Echo Spots installed in other rooms.

The Drop In feature of Echo Show is a cause of privacy concern for some Echo users, unless you have carefully chosen contacts who can "Drop In" with your device. Still others find the **Drop In** feature useful, especially when you have to check on an elderly relative who lives alone. The decision to use the Drop In feature would depend on the user's preference.

The Echo Plus – This Echo family style still has the features of other Echo devices, but with the added functionality as a hub for all your smart home devices.

The device has a built-in Zigbee smart home, which allows the device to work well with Zigbee lights, plugs, light bulbs, in-wall switches and other compatible smart home devices. With the integrated Advanced Audio Distribution Profile (A2DP), the device is great for audio streaming and works from your mobile device to Echo Plus to Bluetooth speaker. Echo Plus is connected to the voice-controlled Alexa, therefore you just speak your command to Alexa for manipulating your smart home devices.

The Echo Plus design retains the cylindrical look of early models of Echo. It has a dimension of 9.2" x 3.3" x 3" and weighs 33.36 oz. Amazon notes that the actual size and weight may differ because of the manufacturing process. The device is equipped with a dual band Wi-Fi connectivity that supports an 802.11 a/b/g/n/ac (2.4 GHz, 5GHz) network.

Voice commands work for Echo plus, but in addition, the device has an action button and a microphone button positioned on top of the cylinder. One button activates Alexa without using the voice command, and the other button mutes the microphone. The device also gives you the choice to manually adjust the volume level of Echo Plus with the rotating ring which you will find near the top portion of the cylinder. A light ring surrounds the upper rim of the cylinder which signals the activity of Echo Plus, including connectivity issues.

As mentioned, the Echo Plus was developed to serve as a hub for your smart home devices. This function was possible in earlier Echo models, but these models need to interface with the product's own smart hub. With the enhanced Echo Plus achieved through the built-in Zigbee wireless protocol, the device is able to bypass the product's hub unit. The built-in Zigbee allows you to speak directly to the speaker, making the system more efficient. Further, the new system eliminates the need for plug sockets for each smart home device as the Echo Plus serves as your bridge for all the smart home devices you own.

The Echo Spot – The Echo spot is another new devise developed by Amazon. It has the most attractive and fancy design of the Echo Family, comes in black or white, equipped with a round screen, and looks like an alarm clock.

The device is quite small and light, just the size of a softball. Its dimension is 4.1" x 3.8" x 3.6" and a weight of 14.8 oz. The device is furnished with a two-band frequency Wi-Fi which supports an 802.11 a/b/g/n (2.4 GHz, 5GHz) networks.

Setting up Echo Spot is easy. Just plug Echo spot to your power supply, connect the device to the internet and you are ready to go. Just like the other Amazon devices, you need an Amazon account to activate Echo Spot.

What Echo Spot can do for you

Echo Spot functions as a high-powered alarm clock and is best positioned on your desk or bedside table. However, it does more than wake you up.

The device is voice-control enabled so you don't have to manually control the Spot. It is hooked to Alexa which enables you to tell her to play your music and watch the lyrics displayed on the screen. Echo Spots also displays playlists, custom stations, and music albums from Amazon music. The Spot is Bluetooth enabled so streaming from other music services is possible with this device.

Like Echo Show, you can watch camera feed from your front door or rooms with installed security cameras.

The Spot has the capability of controlling multiple smart home devices with a single command or schedule an action at a specified time. Just be sure that your smart home devices are compatible with the Echo Spot.

The Echo Spot's screen provides video calls to selected contacts who own Echo Show or has an Alexa app. It also has the Drop In capability so you can connect to your other home devices in an instant.

Echo Spot has a 3.5 mm stereo cable and is also Bluetooth enabled, allowing you to connect the device to your speaker. Connected to your home stereo system, you maximize the voice control capability of Echo Spot and allow you to enjoy music anywhere in your home where Echo devices are installed, like Echo Dot.

The Spot has a night mode that dims the screen light so you don't get bothered with the light when you are about to sleep. You also have the option to set the "do not disturb" mode that sets off the alarm and notification, except for the alarms and the timer. If you want the camera disabled, you can do this on the **Options** menu.

Echo Spot's activity indicators:

- Activating the mute button positioned on top of the device produces a red ring around the screen; a button glows red to indicate the device is no longer listening.
- A small progress bar goes around the screen to indicate active audio or video.
- A blue ring around the screen shows the direction from where you are talking
- Video can be maximized, zoomed in and out, or full display to fit the diameter of the screen.

The Echo Look – This Echo family style is a favorite among fashion bloggers, people who have a passion for new clothes, or those who need help with clothes.

The Echo Look is one of the latest Echo devices of Amazon which is more a camera with Alexa's voice-control technology, and doubles as a speaker. The device can do what the other Echo and Alexa apps offer, but "clothes" is the rationale behind Echo Look's existence. The premise behind Echo Look's functionality is that you don't know which clothing looks good on you; Echo Look helps you decide. To cater to this need, Amazon made Echo Look's main feature a camera that takes floor-length pictures of you, hands-free, and focused on personal style.

Echo Look's Design and Features

The Echo Look device is small, much like your remote control. It's height is 6.3", a width of 2.4", and a depth of 2.4". The device has a built-in 5MP camera and an Intel RealSense SR 300 which gives your photo depth, captures your gestures in different angles, and recognizes your face.

When you purchase an Echo Look, you get a package which contains:

- The Echo Look hardware with a base that can be screwed on and a tripod socket
- 21W power adapter
- A cord that is 7.9 foot long
- A kit to mount Echo Look, should you opt for this approach

The device itself is equipped with:

- A depth-sensor
- Alexa (your voice-control technology)
- A two-band frequency, dual Wi-Fi antenna
- 5 megapixels
- A camera with depth sensors
- A flash which lights from the front, which is useful when in poor lighting conditions
- Four sensitive microphones
- A speaker
- A microphone/a power off button
- Activity indicators

Echo Look costs $200 but its availability is on a per-invitation basis, at least for now. Note, however, that the device has no Bluetooth or auxiliary audio input and output. You also cannot use the Alexa voice remote on the Echo Look. You can, however, use the Alexa app.

Setting up your Echo Look

Setting up your Echo Look is easy, but first, decide where you want to position the device. Since you would be testing and comparing outfit with the Echo Look, the best place would be your bedroom. It is recommended to set the device at shoulder level to achieve the most of a full-length photo.

- Echo Look is downloadable to compatible mobiles, such as Android (Android 5.0 and above) and iOS (iOS 9 up for iPhones 5 and above.)
- When you have decided where to place Echo Look, make sure there are no obstructions between you and the camera (like chairs, top of furniture or other objects.) You should have enough space to make turns freely and pose for full-length photos. You need to be at least 5 feet from your Echo when taking pictures. Position the Echo Look near a power outlet. Check that your room lighting is uniform and that the light does not hit you from behind.
- Plug the power adapter (included in the package) into the Echo Look device and the other end of the adapter to a power socket. When plugged, the light ring at the front of the device turns blue, and turns orange when the device is ready to pair. You will then hear Alexa greet you and enters set up mode. Restart the device when the blue light ring fails to turn orange after five minutes.
- When Echo Look is connected to your Wi-Fi, enter the password and set up the device.
- Sign in to your Amazon account and register Echo Look. You will find a set of instruction in your Echo Look app on how to sign in to your Amazon account. Check to see if

your mobile app and the Echo Look are in the same WI-FI network and that both apps are close to each other.

- Remove the protective wrap and film plastic that cover the device and you are set to start taking your full-length picture.

The Echo Look app

The Echo Look app comes free when you purchase an Echo Look device. You can find the Look in the app store of your mobile phone. The app also contains the photo collection of your clothing (*your Lookbook*), which is useful in keeping track of what is in your closet. The app, further, provides a comparison between two different outfits to help you decide which outfit suits you better (*your Style check*).

In the app's home screen, you find the following options:

- In the home screen, you fill find the latest look you took of your outfit, tips on how to take great photos, and recommendations on what to wear on categorized occasions
- An option for Looks to view your saved photos and videos. In this option, you can filter your favorites
- A style check option where you can compare two outfits to help you decide which looks better on you, taking into consideration the fit, style, color and latest trend.
- The camera option to take photos and videos and includes a live preview.

What Echo Look can do for you

- Take full length pictures of you in your daily outfit just by using a voice command. You get a clear photo from Echo Look because it blurs the background to have a better focus on you. The Look also gives you a live preview of our picture.

- If you wish to see yourself with the outfit in different angles, tell Alexa to take a video (usually for 6 seconds) while you turn and do different poses.
- Offers suggestions learned from your use of daily clothing and provides second opinion on what outfit best suits you.
- Amazon claims to have fashion specialists who can advice you for style and gives you feed back on why a certain outfit is more appropriate for you.
- Helps you curate your clothes for any occasion. The Style Check option has a collection of clothes created based on your personal style which is useful especially for intended future plans, like vacation trips or a date night.
- Echo Look share the same features of other Echo and Alexa apps, like asking for time check, calendar dates, and ordering online.

Tips on using the Echo Look app

When making comparison on Style Check, you do fine with the following:
- *Images are of the same person.* If you are sharing your Echo Look with another person in your household and you tell Alexa to make a comparison of outfit worn by two different persons (such as your image and that of another person), you will receive an *error* feedback.
- *Images are of the same person wearing different outfits.* Remember that what is compared in Echo Look are clothes and not poses. There is no basis for comparison if you wear the same outfit for two images.

The Amazon Tap
The major advantage of the Amazon Tap is its portability. The Tap is a small hardware, with a size at 6.3" x 2.6" x 2.6" and quite light at 16.6 oz. The device comes with a charging cradle which weighs 3.8 oz.

Like other Echo speakers, Alexa is integrated in the system which allows the Tap to do many of the features found in other Echo speakers. The device is wireless and portable, which means you can listen to music even when travelling in your car, stream music, hear current news, and command Alexa for other Alexa voice services.

To activate Amazon Tap, just tap on the microphone button and ask Alexa for your favorite artist or music. You can listen to the device for 9 hours (*8 hours if you are in a hands-free mode*), which is the life span of the battery. Be sure you are connected to a Wi-Fi network through Bluetooth for the Tap to work. Be careful, however, with the device as it is not waterproof. Further, do not expect the sound performance to be as good as the other Echo speakers or other Bluetooth speakers at its price range; Amazon Tap now costs $99.99.

Echo Issues

Using echo is fun and exciting, especially when you are new with the Echo device. It gets even more interesting when installed in your smart home devices. Echo does your bidding with just your voice, at least those commands that you can find in the Echo-Alexa skills.

While others seem content with their Echo device, still others find quirks in the device. These issues, however, are fixable. Here are some reported issues:

The listening echo - The ability of Echo to listen has raised privacy concerns among its users. Echo is equipped with microphones sensitive enough to hear you even when you speak low or wherever you are in the house, and Echo is always listening.

Inconsistent Wi-Fi connection - You can check the status of your WiFi on Echo's LED indicator found at the bottom rear of the device. If your LED indicator shows white, it means your connectivity is good, an orange light means there is no connectivity.

If you see an orange indicator, you can do the following:

- Reboot the router and turn your Echo off and on
- If rebooting fails but all else in the network works, try repositioning your Echo. It is possible that other devices are interfering with your Echo's signal.
- Decongest your network by removing from the network your unused devices.
- If your modem is dual-band, try switching from the 2.4GHz to 5GHz frequency or do the reverse. The 5GHz frequency has less interference, faster speed, less congested, and a more stable connectivity. The 2.4GHz works well with devices located far from the router and when the signal goes through walls.
- Try moving your Echo to a higher location where it will encounter less interference.

Alexa does not connect to other devices - One of Alexa's functionality is to serve as a voice-controlled smart home hub for devices from other manufacturers like SmartThings, Philips, Wink, Insteon, and Honeywell. It is possible that connectivity problems could arise from these devices.

Check for compatibility between Alexa and your other devices. If you find a device that is incompatible with Alexa, you may need a bridge to connect your devices. You can check for compatibility here.

Alexa does not understand your command – When Alexa fails to respond to your command, you will get a response, like "I'm sorry, I don't understand the question." This kind of response can become irritating, especially if you get this often. This irritant, though, can be fixed.

You can try Alexa's voice training tool. It takes time for Alexa to recognize and get used to your voice. Go to **Settings** in the Alexa app, next go to **Voice Training**. You will be instructed to say 25 pre-selected phrases designed to assist Alexa learn your lexicon.

Chapter 6: Watch Original Content with Amazon Prime Video

There are so many videos to view as there are many avid video watchers. If you are already a consumer of Amazon products, you are likely to see the title you are searching from a list published by Amazon. Being able to watch the movie, a favorite TV show, listen to current news, or watch a program is another thing.

Videos are categorized according to the type and quality of videos. You have three options to stream content using your Amazon fire stick: Prime video, Amazon Video, and Amazon Channels. This chapter is about Amazon Prime and viewing Amazon Prime Video contents.

What is Amazon Prime

Amazon Prime is a paid service which enables the user to access much of Amazon services, such as streaming videos, games, music, e-books, and other services with added perks like 2-day free shipping and discounts.

A member of the Amazon Prime is entitled to the following services:

- *2-day shipping free* – A benefit which was originally intended to attract membership to Amazon Prime, but led to the rise of Amazon Prime Video. With this benefit, you get one to two days delivery of practically unlimited Amazon eligible items at no cost. If fast delivery is not a concern, you can opt for a "no-rush delivery", and in return, you get a promotional credit.

  Some products, however, are not eligible for fast delivery, such as:
  o Products from Amazon's marketplace sellers
  o Magazine subscriptions

- o Gift cards that are personalized
- o International addresses and in US territories, protectorates, or possessions (except Puerto Rico)

- *Amazon Prime Video* – gives you access and stream thousands of original movies, TV programs and shows, some of which are exclusive. You can also download and enjoy watching these contents offline. You get these benefits as a member of Amazon Prime, however, if you have no intention of becoming an Amazon Prime member, you still can subscribe to Amazon Prime Video as an individual service and enjoy its contents.

- *Amazon Channels* – you have access to additional paid TV channels and other video contents contracted with other third party channels, though this benefit is available only to Prime members. This benefit is your niche program, like Discovery Channel for one.

- *Prime Photos* – this benefit gives you unlimited cloud storage for your photos, and additional 5 GB for your videos and documents. Cloud storage provides the assurance that your photos and videos are secure and you can retrieve them at will.

- *Prime Music* – This benefit is a new feature at Amazon Prime, but one that is fast improving and growing. This is Amazon's equivalent of Spotify which gives you access to thousands of song titles.

- *Amazon Music Unlimited* – this feature is different from Prime Music. With Amazon Music Unlimited, you get much more songs (40 million songs to Prime Music's 2 million) that are free for Prime members but paid for non-members. If becoming a Prime member is of no interest to you, you can subscribe to Amazon Music Unlimited streaming service only.

- *Prime Early Access* – if you are a Prime member and love bargains, this feature will make you happy. With Prime Early Access, you get a head start of 30 minutes in viewing and ordering items out for flash sales before non-Prime members. What's more, if you are a reader you will have access to Kindle Owners' Lending Library and Kindle First.

- *Amazon Prime Pantry* – this benefit provides access to everyday home essentials, like groceries and household products, at a low price with a fixed delivery fee of $5.99 per box. With purchases that exceed 5, boxes, delivery is free.

- *Amazon Household* – this benefit allows you to share delivery with another adult in your household and split the cost of delivery. You can also share Prime Video and Kindle Owners' Library.

- *Prime Reading* – This benefit allows you to download unlimited comics, books, and magazines from Amazon's library which contains 1000 or more holdings. If you are an existing Prime member, you can keep 10 titles each transaction, and should you need another, simply return one and get another. For new members, the subscriber needs to return the borrowed item and get another one.

- *Amazon Restaurants* – If you order food through Amazon restaurant with cost not lower than $20, you get the food delivered within an hour if you live in Orlando, Manhattan,

Los Angeles and 17 more metro areas. You need to check if an Amazon restaurant is available in your locality.

- *Amazon Elements* – This feature is exclusive for Prime members which allows them to access Amazon's line of premium organic products, which include vitamins and baby wipes.
- *Twitch prime* – The latest service added to the Amazon Prime gives you discounts on games, ad-free viewing if you attach your Amazon Prime account to Twitch.tv, and free channel subscription each month.

- *Amazon Dash* – Amazon dash is an ordering and reordering service which allows you to order consumer goods through the web. Dash buttons are exclusive for the Prime members. Dash Buttons are free, including fast delivery for products ordered, so you can add as many buttons depending on your favorite products.

- Membership to Amazon Prime offers convenience, savings through discounts, fast deliveries, and bonuses. One such bonus is the Prime Wardrobe where you order items from Amazon with no delivery charge. If you decide to keep three to four items, you get 100% off and 20% off if you keep five items.

Further, with Amazon Prime you are certain to see more features and benefits to come since Amazon keeps adding them.

Amazon Prime Video

Amazon Prime video's introduction to the market was to draw in membership to Amazon Prime. As it turned out, Amazon Prime Video became its own magnet as a new option for streaming Amazon contents. Not only was Amazon Prime Video a success, it paved the way to become a competition for traditional studios and existing streaming services.

Amazon Prime Video is a streaming service exclusive for Amazon Prime members. As a member of Amazon Prime or if you subscribe to Amazon Prime Video, you become eligible for a 30-day trial, share Amazon Prime Video content to an eligible adult member of your household, and have ready access to a multitude of Prime Video titles free of charge.

You can judge the quality of Amazon Prime Video's collection with its inclusion of award-winning originals, like *Manchester by the Sea, The Grand Tour, The Man in the High Castle, and Mozart in the Jungle.*

Through Prime Video, you can watch and subscribe to Amazon Channels which features HBO Showtime, Starz, and PBS Kids.

Note, however, that a membership to Amazon Prime Video alone will not entitle you to the 2-day shipping perk and other benefits available to Amazon Prime members. Both are paid membership, but Amazon Prime Video is a plan paid on a monthly basis.

How to maximize your Amazon Prime Video viewing

- Download your TV show or movie and watch offline at your time and convenience. Streaming content requires an internet connection, which may not be available when you are on the road or any place where the wireless connection is not available. You will appreciate this feature when, for instance you are on the road with your kids. The children can watch a movie while your drive.

  For you fire stick, you can download your selection to android phones and tablets. All you need to do is direct the arrow downward (not the play button) and it will display the time period for viewing.

- Enjoy fun facts with X-ray. Amazon is behind the Internet Movie Database (IMDb) which makes it possible for the integration of IMDb to Prime video thru X-ray. You, therefore, can get trivia, footages of behind-the-scenes, information on cast and crew of your favorite TV shows, programs, or movies. If these contents support X-ray, (check the player for the X-ray icon) the icon will pause the movie and resume when you want to continue.

- Browse for specific themes. If you are not sure of the content you would like to watch, you tend to go to the **Recently Added** or **Recommended** sections. It would be easier if you search for themes, like Romance TV, Comedy TV, Anime TV, and more thematic categories. Another way is to go to the search tab and enter a theme or, for example Zombie. Your search for Zombie will return 100 or more of zombie-related movies or TV shows.

- Use voice command to search for your content. Your Amazon fire stick is equipped with Alexa voice control which allows you to talk to your phone directly and ask for the item. A convenient feature, especially when you are driving.

- Set your parental control. This feature is best if you have children and what they watch on TV in your absence worries you. Parental control is built into the fire stick service. Parental control requires your PIN which prevents unauthorized persons to access the fire stick's contents.

- Use enabled closed captioning. There are advantages for closed captioning and subtitles. This feature is designed for those who are deaf or have difficulty in hearing. They still can enjoy viewing the fire stick content through this feature. There could also be instances where you need to tone the volume down or shut audio completely. Another advantage is for users who are more comfortable reading content in their mother tongue.

Chapter 7: Video Content on Demand through Amazon Video

With several streaming services in one company and with the different names given to these streaming services, it could be confusing for a beginner in Amazon video products. Take for instance two streaming services, the Amazon Prime Video and the Amazon Video; users tend to confuse the two products as one and the same. The two products, however, are different with the services they provide.

The difference between Amazon Prime Video and Amazon Video

Amazon Prime Video is available only to Prime members, while the Amazon Video is available to both Prime members and non-Prime members. With Amazon Prime Video, you can stream as much as you can. As a member, all Prime Video contents are already paid for by Amazon Prime.

With Amazon Video, you buy or rent a title. Because titles are paid for individually rather than by a flat fee, you get access to more content, which also happens to be the latest and best titles in the entertainment industry. With the Amazon Video, therefore, you can watch your favorite movie or TV show on demand. All you need is an Amazon Prime account and a compatible device with a good internet connection.

Since Amazon Video is a standalone streaming service, you can access it through:

- Your desktop's web browser
- Set-top boxes of other streaming service providers
- Blu-Ray players
- Amazon Fire TV
- Amazon Fire Stick

- iOS devices
- Android devices
- Fire tablets
- Fire phone

To activate the Amazon Video, however, you need to have an Amazon account. If you already have an account, sign in to access **Your Video Library**, buy or rent titles, and more menu options. If this is your first to sign in and needs help, you can check <u>here</u>.

1-click ordering and payment

You can rent or buy a Prime video title from any registered device you have and pay through Amazon's 1-click order and payment service. These purchased or rented titles are stored in **Your Video Library** which is in your device.
When you make your initial order and enter your mode of payment, 1-click ordering is automatically activated. With 1-click ordering, you bypass the shopping cart and place an order directly. Upon clicking on **Buy now with 1-click,** your purchase is charged automatically to your Amazon account and the item shipped to the address entered in your registration.

How to rent or buy a video title

- From your computer's web browser, open the Prime video. You can also open the Prime Video from any of your connected device.
- Once you are in the Prime Video page, you can search for a title or browse the featured categories
- To view the movie details, select a title
- Select **Rent** or **Buy**
- Confirm the purchase
- Upon completion of the order, select **Watch Now** for playback to begin.

The option **Buy** means you now own the title and is kept in **Your Video Library**. Since you own the title, you can retrieve the movie from your library and watch the movie anytime you want. On the other hand, when you **Rent** a title, the title is stored in Your Video Library for the duration of the rental period. You can watch the movie at anytime within the rental period. When the rental period lapses the title is removed automatically from the list.

If the video fails to play or is not in **Your Video Library**, check for the following:

- Order status – go to your digital order to make sure you have completed your order. You might have accidentally skipped or missed an entry.
- Payment settings – Go over the information you supplied in the 1-click payment and check if you have entered all requested information.
- Accidental orders – There are times when you make accidental orders. You can cancel accidental orders within 48 hours after purchase, and only if you have not started downloading or streaming the movie.

Watching First Episodes for Free

Amazon Video allows free streaming of TV show's first episodes from your compatible devices. Free first episodes, though, comes with advertising breaks before and during playbacks.

Some of the compatible devices:

- Roku
- Xbox One
- Fire tablets (excluding Kindle Fire 1st generation)
- Play Station3 and 4
- iPhone, iPad, & iPod touch
- Fire phone

Chapter 8: Curate your own Niche Video Content in Amazon Channels

You might wonder why have another streaming service when there already are two streaming services in one gateway, the Prime Video and the Amazon Video? What makes Amazon Channels special and distinct from the other two?

If you recall, one of the Amazon fire stick's added feature is the Advanced Streaming and Prediction system (ASAP). ASAP collects data on the viewers' behavior and preferences in video content, which data collected and analyzed allow the system to predict a user's favorite show and buffers it before the user actually selects the show.

The system also has the ability to provide information on what gaps still exist between user preferences and the services provided. This gap is what Amazon Channels is all about.

What is Amazon Channels?

While it is true that Prime Video provides its members with thousands of video content, some of these contents are dependent on third-party contracts. Amazon Channels cuts through the limitations you encounter with other streaming services by giving you direct access to your favorite channels. Amazon Channels, in effect, is your portal to subscribe to other specialized streaming services.

You get to understand the Amazon channels if you imagine it as a way to have a more managed and customized list of video content to stream. A strong appeal of Amazon Channels is its *niche programming options*. Niche programming could be the answer to users' preferences for specialist content, which often are difficult to track down from niche providers.

With Amazon Channels, you only pay for the content you like and ignore those that have no use for you. However, Amazon Channels provides a wide array of niche programming to choose, from Discovery channel to fitness channels. The subscription fee for individual channel varies, depending on the streaming service you are subscribing to.

For instance, access to HBO goes with a monthly fee of $14.99 and a 7-day trial period. A subscription to PBS kids requires a monthly fee of $4.99 with a 7-day trial period.

Access to Amazon Channels, though, requires you to be a member of Amazon Prime. In addition to Amazon Prime membership, you become eligible if you are a member of any of the following:

- Annual Prime Student membership
- Prime student free trial
- Amazon Prime free review
- 30-day Amazon Prime free trial
- 30-day Amazon Prime Fresh free trial
- Amazon Household shared Prime Benefits

Should you wish to avail of Amazon Channels, you are provided with a free 30-trial period, which gives you the advantage of deciding if Amazon Channels is for you or if the niche channel is to your liking. If you eventually decide to access subscriptions through Amazon Channels and change your mind at a later date, you can cancel anytime with no cancellation fee if you are a member of Amazon Prime.

There are limits to what you can subscribe; following are excluded from eligibility:
- Subscription from other premium channels or satellite providers
- Direct purchase of standalone subscriptions from other service providers
- You cannot share Amazon Channel subscriptions across Amazon accounts

- Sharing of Amazon Channels with Amazon Household profiles is also not allowed.

Difference of Amazon Channels from Prime Video and Amazon Video

Having three streaming services in one company is bound to create confusion among users. There is a reason for the development of each streaming service, though you cannot discount the goal of directing users to patronize Amazon products. Why not, if you get choice products at low prices and obtained with ease and convenience?

The brief descriptions of Prime Video and Amazon Video below will show you how each streaming service differ from each other and from Amazon Channels. Hopefully, this will guide you to search for an appropriate streaming service for your entertainment, information, and gaming needs.

Prime Video – a streaming service which comes with membership to Amazon Prime, giving you access to all original content (*like Man in the Castle, Bosch, and Mozart in the Jungle*), TV series and movie titles (like *Girls, Downtown Abbey, and the American*), and movies (*like Breathe, Good Time, and Ex Machine*). More TV series and movie titles are added to satisfy film lovers.

Amazon Video – this streaming service gives users a repository of paid-for content, some of which are free to stream for Amazon Prime members. If you are a Prime member and you browse through the list of content, you will know which content is free for streaming. Like the Prime Video, content for Amazon Video are regularly updated with new TV series and movie titles.

Watch Amazon Channels

You may have an Amazon account which makes you eligible to access Amazon Channels. However, you still need to subscribe to your favorite channel if you want to watch it through Amazon Channels.

To watch your favorite channel, go to **Prime Video** and search for **Your Subscription**. Once you have found the channel you are looking for, browse the featured movies, TV shows, or you can browse the programming by category.

If you are looking for a specific movie to watch or a TV program, go to the **Ways to Watch** or **Refine** options and then **Subscriptions**. This selection approach filters video categories and shows results of titles you can view with your Channels. When you find one you would want to watch hit the **Watch Now** option from the details of the video to start watching the video.

Tip: Select Channels that include offers of downloads for TV shows and movies in your active subscriptions. Select eligible titles you can download and watch offline. Check to see if a Download button is included in the video details.

Watch Live video through Amazon Channels

Look for Channel subscriptions that feature **Watch Live** option. This option allows you to live stream programs to your compatible devices simultaneously with its broadcast on TV. Channels with Watch Live option usually update programs and show what is now live on each of the subscription's TV channels.

To watch the live stream, hit **Play** to start streaming. You can do the following during the streaming:
- Pause the stream
- Go forward or back
- Rewind for up to 60 minutes
- Jump to live (when streaming is paused or rewinding)

Difference of Amazon Channels from Netflix and Hulu

If you have experienced watching video content from Netflix or Hulu, it makes you wonder what makes Amazon distinct from the two.

Netflix and Hulu are standalone streaming services paid with a flat fee. Subscribing to either Netflix or Hulu makes you eligible to view all contents of each streaming service. The content offered by each are sourced from different streaming providers. Contents, however, are rotated within the subscription period, in accordance to the content-distribution agreement entered into with content providers.

Amazon Channels, on the other hand, contains an array of content streaming services which eligible Prime members can subscribe to through content providers. You can consider Amazon Channels as a hub where you can subscribe to your favorite content through Amazon Video. Amazon handles subscription payments for you.

Chapter 9: Enjoy Unlimited Photo and Personal Video Storage and Sharing

Who would not want to take photos of yourself, the family, friends, and pets during happy (and the not-so-happy) moments? And to save these photos as memories that you can share with friends or look back to in the future? Then, come the time when you have to remove older photos to save space in your digital device to make ways for new ones. Choosing which to delete could be a tough task.

With the Prime Photo and Personal Video app, saving and storing photos and personal videos are no longer a problem for those who love taking and storing pictures.

What is Prime Photo?

Prime Photo is an extra feature which is pre-installed in your Amazon Fire Stick and gives you unlimited storage capacity plus 5GB of storage for your videos, documents, and other files. With Prime Photo, you can share photos filed in the Family Vault with five other members of the Household at no additional cost.

What Prime Photo can do for you

- View your pictures and personal videos that are less than 20 minutes long
- Save unlimited photos and share them on mobiles, desktop, and tablets
- Share unlimited storage with a maximum of 5 other users in the Amazon Household
- Collect pictures in the Family Vault
- Back up your photos with the Prime Photo app
- Access your photos across devices, such as desktop, tablet, mobile anywhere you are

- Set photos from the Family Vault as Screen Savers

How to Back up Photos with your Prime Photo

You may already have backup support for your saved photos and videos. But using unlimited storage for backup is definitely an advantage that should not be ignored.

Whatever device you save your photos in, it is quite simple to upload your photos to the Prime Photo app. You can store your photos in three ways:

- Manual upload
- photos app for Windows and Mac computers
- mobile apps for iOS and android

Whatever method you choose to upload your photos, you need to go to your Prime Photo account and register or sign in.

- *Manual back up*

- Sign in to your Prime Photo account or register a new account if your are new to Prime Photos
- When you have opened your Prime Photo account, select **Upload Photos.** This option will allow you to use your operating system's file explorer and select photos to upload
- Alternatively, you can drag and drop selected photos directly to your browser's pane.

An upload meter appears to indicate upload progress. When completed, you can start browsing your pictures.

Latest version of Prime Photos has improved much compared to its earlier versions. Prime Photo is now able to recognize faces and contexts. Take note of the "People" and "Things" Tags and use it to facilitate your search of photos. For instance, you can search for your kid under "People" and specify Lawn under "Things" and you will be given pictures of your child playing on your lawn.

Backup for Desktop App

Dragging and dropping photos may not be a practical means to upload photos if you have hundreds of photos stored. A more convenient way is the Desktop app which is compatible with Window 8, Windows 10, and Windows 7.

With the Desktop app installed on your computer, you can:
- Upload as many files and folders instantly
- Download photos to your computer
- Store you photos, files, and other documents safely
- View photos on your desktop
- Convert names of folders into album names

How to back up photos using the Desktop app

- Sign in to your account
- When signing in is complete, you will receive a prompt requesting you to confirm the folder you would like to use as syncing folder.

  When you install the Desktop App, a default folder is created under your user directory with the name "Amazon Drive." You can change the name later. Leaving the default folder as is gives you the opportunity to explore the file syncing by loading folders as you go along before you start syncing them. You can then check if the folders are working as you want them to.
- Click "Next" and you get a prompt to sync folders between your Amazon Drive account and your computer. It is recommended that you skip this step for now. It will not affect the backup process.
- The last step is where the Desktop app gives you a key that will allow you to read the interface for Amazon Drive, allowing the Drive app to settle in your system tray, ready to receive files you will upload.

Check your backup process by uploading some test folders or photos in the sync directory and observe how the uploading works.

Go to your Prime Photo web dashboard and you will see the photos you uploaded. Note that:

- Prime Photo scans your Amazon Drive folder for photos and displays them on the dashboard according to dates taken, and organized according to Tags or categories, like People and Things.
- Prime Photos does not carry the labels or names in the directory you may have attached to your folders before the backup process. If you choose for Prime Photo to use your directory names, in addition to Prime Photos categories, you will have to do some work on the Prime Photo dashboard.
- If your purpose of uploading your photos is for backup purposes only, you need not change the directory name nor that of Prime Photo directory. The Desktop app keeps your photos with the original directory name even if Prime Photos fail to recognize your directory by default.

Backup for Mobile apps

It is the reality today that most people use the phone to take pictures than in any other gadgets. Backing up your mobile is even more important that phones tend to get lost, broken, or stolen than computers.

To start backing up your mobile photos, download the Prime Photos app to your android or iPhone, install it, and log in to your Prime Photos account. You will receive a prompt allowing Prime Photos to access your photos; confirm the request.

Your concern at this point is whether to let Prime Photos to upload your picture automatically or you might want to do it manually. When you have decided, you can click "Ok" or "Not Now" so you can have the opportunity to explore the app before you allow Prime Photos to upload your mobile pictures.

More Features for the Prime Photos

Continuous development of the Prime Photos resulted to new features added giving users a new kind of experience with the Prime Photos app: the Alexa voice control technology and the Family Vault. These features are integrated in your Amazon Fire Stick.

Alexa

If your device has an Alexa-enabled system, it is easy for you to view your photos. Simply ask Alexa to display your photos appear. You can ask Alexa to show pictures from your various albums and photos taken on specific days, weeks or months. Or you may want to retrieve photos taken at a certain location, with your friends, or with your favorite pet – simply ask Alexa and you will have your pictures displayed.

Family Vault

This is a feature that family members will enjoy. Family Vault is a group-sharing feature of Prime Photos which allow up to five members of the family to add pictures to the vault and which all can access anytime. You can ask Alexa to show photos or a slide show of photos in your Family Vault which all members can watch together. Imagine the fun family members will have recalling memories of past experiences.

Storing Raw Images

This feature is not highlighted in Prime Photos but may best be appreciated by photographers. Storing raw file images are stored in Prime Photos free allowance. Raw images are images camera sensors which have not gone through compression, or perhaps with only light compression. Photographers see the advantage of raw files which keep the images' dynamic range. Raw files also allow for post-processing work to compensate for the images' under- or overexposure.

Since Prime Photos allow storing of jpegs and raw files, the feature is great news for photographers or one whose hobby it is to take and edit pictures in the raw.

Chapter 10: Prime Music and Amazon Unlimited Music

Streaming music is not a stranger to music lovers. The music streaming craze has been going on since the 2000's. What makes music streaming today different from the early years is in the quality of music. From mp3 of the early 2000's, it went through CD quality, and now to higher quality music through enhanced music streams developed by streaming services, and the hardware used to deliver those streams to mobiles, tablets, and computers.

Amazon Prime Music may be a latecomer in music streaming, but this does not mean being behind in quality of streaming services and content. With continued attention to quality of application and content updates and upgrades, Amazon is catching on with its two music streaming services, the *Prime Music* and *Music Unlimited*.

What is Amazon Prime Music?

Prime Music is an ads-free extra feature of Amazon Prime offered to members which gives them access to millions of curated songs in its Prime Playlists at no additional costs.

When you sign on to Prime Music, you get:

- Two-day shipping for free
- Prime Video
- Kindle Owner's Library
- Audio streams of Bundesliga 1plus its conferences in English (this a new feature added to Prime Music)
- Collection of songs curated by Prime Music's experts into Playlists

- Create your Personal Playlist
- Access to Prime Stations which feature uninterrupted music and unlimited skips
- Play Prime Music offline

You can play your music with compatible devices, such as:
- Amazon Echo
- Amazon Music for web
- iOS devices
- PC and Mac computers
- Fire phone and tablets
- Amazon Fire Stick/Amazon Fire TV
- HEOS devices
- Bose Sound Touch System
- Bluesound and Sonos devices
- Play-Fi devices

What makes Amazon Prime Music a favored choice are the additional features that gives it the edge over other streaming devices:

- *Cheap subscription rate.* Prime Music subscription is cheaper than other streaming services at $8.25 per month. Prime Music offers student-members with a 30-day trial period and a 50% discount at the end of the trial period
- *Easy to navigate.* Prime Music's design is minimalist and straightforward, which makes it easy to control with just a few clicks whatever device you are using.
- *Audio quality.* Bit-rate is the rate per second that music is transmitted to your digital network. Prime Music player delivers your music from a range of 48 kbps to 320 kbps (the usual standard being 256 kbps) in four settings:

  o Low – has the lowest bit-rate and the least bandwidth
  o Medium – a balance between bit-rate and bandwidth use

- o High – has the highest bit-rate and the most bandwidth
- o Auto – bit-rate changes depending the quality of your network

- *Add your purchased songs.* A missing feature in other music streaming services, Prime Music allows you to create your personal playlist and add songs you bought or already exist in your music directory. Adding music is simple; just upload the bought music to your Amazon Prime account. And, you do not have to worry about playback failure because Prime Music synchronizes your personal music library across all Prime Music apps.

How to locate your Prime Music

Finding your music could be a task for a beginner in Prime Music. But, compatible music device, locating your music is easy.

For eligible Prime members, go to the Amazon music menu and select **Browse**. You will then find featured music, new releases, recommended titles, streaming stations, and Playlists.

Under the **More Options** menu, you will find three vertical dots which indicate you can add albums and Playlists, including your personal music library. If you are new to Prime Music, you can do the adding function for later so you can explore more on the functionalities of Prime Music.

Under **My Music** in the navigation bar, you will find the music you added, purchased, or imported to Prime Music. These songs are categorized according to songs, artists, albums, or according to mood. If you happen to be impatient locating your music, go to **Recent** under the navigation bar for a quick find.

If you come across a song title that is greyed and you cannot access it, the greyed title could mean any of the following:

- *No longer available.* Prime Music always changes its collection of songs and albums to give way to new titles. Often, Prime Music remove song titles. Even when removed and no longer available, they still get displayed under My Music.

  What to do: You can purchase the title of your missed music and add it to your personal music library. Or if you a subscriber of Music Unlimited, you can access it there if the song is available.

- *Expiration of Prime membership.* When your Prime membership lapses, you will lose your access to Prime Music, though the song titles still get displayed in **My Music.** You will regain access to Prime Music if you activate your account.

- *Unused music for 30 days.* You will lose access to music downloaded through Amazon Music app or lose offline playback if you have not played the music while connected to a wireless network within 30 days. Though no longer accessible, you will still see the titles as greyed in **My Music**.

  What to do: If the song title is still available at the Prime Music catalog, you can have access to it again through the Amazon Music App. Download the music from the Amazon Music app to regain access. Note that it may take some time to download the music and another few minutes before you can regain access to the music.

  Note also that the music you downloaded through Prime Music gets deleted once you sign off from Amazon Music app.

Downloading Prime Music for Offline Playback

Downloading for offline playback is a favorite feature of music lovers, especially if you are nowhere near a wireless connection or when traveling. Prime Music songs are available for offline playback on Amazon Music for Androids, Amazon Music for iOS, and on Fire tablets. You cannot, however, download Prime music on computers.

Simple steps to download Prime Music (for androids and iOS):

- Select the song, album or playlist you want to download
- Go to the **More Options** menu indicated by the three vertical dots icon
- Tap the **Download** option
- Open **My Music.** You will find a checkmark beside your downloaded music
- Another way to open your downloaded music is to go to **Offline Music Mode** from **Settings.** The **Offline Music Mode** will display only the music downloaded and that is available for offline playback.
- For quick access to your downloads, select **Recent** under your Amazon Music menu and choose **Recently Downloaded Songs**

For downloading on tablets, simply select the music you want to download, press and hold, and from the menu tap **Download**. If you want to share music with other people, go to **More Options** menu then **Share.** You can then choose how you want to share your music or you can simply copy and share the link. Note, however, that the Share functions only if the recipient has an active Amazon Music Prime or Music Unlimited subscription.

What is Amazon Music Unlimited?

The Amazon Music Unlimited is another ads-free music streaming service offered by Amazon. Music Unlimited is similar to Prime Music, but offers more features and more song titles than Prime Music. Amazon claims that with Music Unlimited, an eligible subscriber gets access to "tens of millions of track music", which is basically the major difference from Prime Music with 2,000 song titles.

Music Unlimited includes the voice-control Alexa which gives you a convenient way of access to your music. Just give your command to Alexa for a specific song title, artist, or album and Alexa plays it back for you. It is not a problem if you happen to forget the title of a song. You can sing a tune and Alexa will recognize the song and play it back. Alexa is also able to play music you request by decade, genre, or mood.

Amazon Music Unlimited shares much the same features with Prime Music, including the ways to download and play music.

On Stations of Music Unlimited

Amazon Music Stations are your personalized streaming music that plays ads-free music. You will find Stations under **Browse** from your **Amazon Music menu**. Selecting Stations will display an array of Stations categorized according to artists, popular titles, genre, and mood. Select the Station you want to listen to and select **Play** to start streaming.

With Stations, you can have unlimited plays and skips, pause and resume playbacks, play previously played songs, and add the currently played song to one of your personal playlists or to **My Music**.

Stations allows you to save ratings which customizes your Stations playback. Just choose the **Thumbs Up** icon under your playback controls if you want to hear more of the currently played song or if you want more music like it. The **Thumbs Down** icon stops the song from playing and removes it from the song rotation of the Stations.

Subscription plans for Music Unlimited

Music Unlimited offers several subscription plans, each with its distinct purpose, for someone who wish to have access to the millions of track music. Each plan is briefly presented below to help you decide which is appropriate for your purpose:

Individual subscription plan – this plan is for you if your intention is to have access to Amazon Music Unlimited on all of our compatible devices – PC or Mac, tablet, smartphone, Fire Stick and Fire TV, and Amazon Echo.

Family Plan - Choose this plan is you want to save on subscription cost. Up to 6 family members can join the Family Plan and listen to Music Unlimited at the same time. Family members included in the Family plan get the benefits of an Individual Plan, personalized recommendations, and playlists.

Echo Plan – gives you exclusive listening to Amazon Music Unlimited on Echo devices, such as Echo Dot, Echo Look, Echo Show, and Amazon Tap. Should you choose to, you can upgrade to the Individual Plan if you want to listen to more devices than just your Echo. Upgrading can be done through Alexa by giving the command for Alexa to upgrade your Music Unlimited subscription. Another way to upgrade is to go to **Your Amazon Music Settings**.

Amazon continues to update and upgrade its two music streaming services. You can, therefore, expect the releases of latest music by different popular artists, better sound quality, and delivery services to eligible subscribers.

Chapter 11: Twitch Prime for Gamers

"Broadcasting and watching gameplay is a global phenomenon and Twitch has built a platform that brings together tens of millions of people who watch billions of games each month."

Jeff Bezos, Amazon Founder and Chief Executive

When Amazon acquired Twitch to the tune of $1 billion, many people wondered why Amazon would bother buying a service which is more a spectator's thing than anything else.

Unknown to many people, and as Jeff Bezos said, broadcasting games and watching players play games are fast becoming a global phenomenon. What Amazon, in effect, did was to capture the vast number of passive spectators to live streaming of games. Much like the spectators of sports played on arenas, quite a significant number of people consider watching players play on video games as fun and exciting.

What is Twitch Prime

Twitch is a platform for live video streaming of games owned by Twitch Interactive, now a subsidiary of Amazon. As Amazon's subsidiary, Twitch is now included in Amazon Prime and Prime Video memberships. Twitch provides its viewers or users premium experience with its games and in-game content. It also includes a 30-days free channel subscription which a user can use on any third-party channels of Affiliate channels. Added features provided are ads-free viewing, emotes which are exclusive on Twitch, and chat badge.

What you gain from Twitch Prime membership

- *Ads-free viewing experience during broadcast.* You get to enjoy watching uninterrupted live streaming of your favorite games or channels. Viewing may be ads-free but Twitch Partners still gain revenues from views of Premium members.
- *Twitch Channel Subscription.* If you are an active Prime member, you get a 30-day free channel subscription which includes additional perks, such as emoticons, chat privileges, and many more. One you activate your Prime membership, you can access your free Twitch Channel Subscription.
- *Access to Game content.* You can access and select your favorite game and in-game content free. Twitch regularly updates its selection of in-game loot and video games. You can view offers from **Crown**.
- *Exclusive Emoticons.* Emoticons which are exclusive to Twitch are provided for Prime and Turbo members, such as KappaHD and ScaredyCat, to mention a few.
- *More Chat Color Options.* You can choose your chat color any time just by toggling three sliders. If you want to change to another color, go to your Prime settings.
- *Chat Badge exclusive for Prime members.* A unique and exclusive badge for Prime members which you earn each time you show support and for which you earn recognition.

Subscribing to Twitch Prime

Subscribing for live game streaming not only makes you a member of a gaming channel or streaming service, but shows your support for your favorite streamer. When you subscribe to Twitch Prime, the benefit goes both ways: you as the subscriber gains digital rewards like emoticons, badges, and a premium viewing experience, while the streamer gets a recurring source of income.

When you subscribe to Twitch Prime, you will be given four options and you choose what options apply to you:

Option 1 - If you are a current Twitch Turbo user, you will be requested to unsubscribe from Twitch Turbo. By cancelling your Twitch Turbo subscription, you avoid paying double subscription fees. To cancel your Twitch Turbo subscription go to your Turbo Tab from settings and click **Don't Renew** that appears on the center of the page. Next, go to your billing schedule and click **Don't Renew**.

Option 2 – If you are a current Amazon Prime member, you can access your Twitch Prime. Connect the two accounts:
   o Go to your Twitch Prime.com
   o Click and connect your Twitch account to Amazon Prime account
   o Once connected, you automatically gain access to Twitch Prime and get all the benefits offered by Twitch Prime

Option 3 - If you are neither a Twitch Prime nor an Amazon Prime member, before you subscribe to the Amazon Prime, check if for your country of residence. You will find this in the right corner at the top of the sign-up page. After checking your residence country, sign in or create an Amazon account. Next step is to connect your Amazon Prime account with the Twitch Prime account to avail of the benefits.

Option 4 – If you have an existing Prime Video membership but your residence is in a country not found in those listed at the top of the sign up page, you still can register for a Twitch Prime subscription. As a member of the Amazon Prime Video, you can obtain the Twitch Prime by connecting your Twitch prime account to Amazon Prime Video. Go to twitchprime.com and click **Start Your Free Trial.** The, connect your Prime Video account to your Twitch Prime account to avail of the benefits.

Option 5 – If you do not belong to any of the first four options, follow the following steps:

- o   Go to twitchprime.com and set your country of residence to **Prime Video Worldwide Plan**
- o   Sign in or create your Amazon Prime Video account
- o   Fill in billing address and mode of payment details; start your Prime Video membership
- o   Log in to the created Amazon account
- o   Log in to your Twitch Prime account
- o   Connect your Amazon account to your twitch prime account and avail of your benefits

Recently, Amazon launched a new Twitch program which gives away free games. This program is free for Twitch Prime Members where each member received a collection of free games the member can keep, and this is regularly handed each month.

Chapter 12: Have Family Fun Sharing Prime Contents with Amazon Household

It is highly likely that in a family household, two or more members would be holding an Amazon account. With each member having multiple accounts, things could become pricey and somehow not practical. Why buy the same thing when you can share it. To give an example, you can share Kindle books instead of buying more.

Sharing accounts is what Amazon household is for; it is for families living in the same residence. Think how much a family saves with the Amazon Household and who the family could enjoy sharing the Prime benefits, instead of members having individual Amazon accounts.

What is Amazon Household?

Amazon household is one of many features you get when you join the membership plan of the Amazon Prime. With Amazon Household, you are able to share your Amazon benefits with another adult in your family household, including teens and children. The adults can share Prime benefits, use the Amazon's Family Library digital content, manage the teens and children profile in the household. Teens can also share some Prime benefits.

Amazon Household can admit up to 10 members of the family:
- Two adults aged 18 and over with each owning an Amazon account
- Fourteen profiles, this is limited to ages 13 to 17. Teens are allowed to share Prime Benefits, if parents are members of Amazon Prime.
- Four child profiles aged 12 and below. Children in the Amazon Household can use Amazon experience focused on children, like the Amazon Free Time. Children profiles, though, are not eligible for shopping on Amazon. Adding a

child or children to the Household gives parents control over their children's use of Fire tablets, Fire TV, and what they read on Kindle.

Creating a Household

 If you have a family and hold an Amazon account, you can create an Amazon Household using your account. To add another adult, both need to be present so they can verify their accounts together. When adding a teen to the Amazon Household, teen acceptance of the parent's invitation is necessary to establish the teen's credentials for login purposes.

What you need to know before you create a household account:

- You need an Amazon Prime account before you can share your Prime access.
- You cannot share Prime access to someone in your family household with discounted Student Prime Account. For that someone to qualify for Prime access, you will have to pay the full Prime rate.
- You are not eligible for Amazon Household if you are already a guest on another person's Prime account
- The other adult of your household should have a separate login and password. Children in will not need separate accounts as their membership is profile-based considered as sub-categories of the parent's accounts.
- Amazon Household is ideal for spouses. If you link another adult to your account, you will be exposing your billing and payment information to that other adult, giving them access to your credit cards associated with your account. It is best to keep membership to the Amazon Household within the family.
- When you remove an adult from the Household or you leave the Household, you cannot create another Household nor join another Amazon Household for 180 days.

Setting up the Amazon Household

- Make sure the other adult is with you when you create the Amazon Household. You will need the presence of the other adult for verification purposes. You don't need the presence of children since their accounts are based on the account holder.
- Go to **Manage Your Household** page, select **Add Adult** and click it.
- You will get a prompt to either:
  - Have the other adult login to their Amazon Prime account
  - Create a new account
- When login is complete, select "We agree to share..." and click **Create Household**
- The next page prompts you to check which items to share (*games, audiobooks, ebooks*)
- The next step is a prompt to set the default credit or debit card for each adult. This is part of Prime Video sharing rules before you can use instant streaming or sharing of contents.
- Once you have completed the default payment, you will be directed to the main Amazon Household page.
- On the left side of the Amazon Household page, you can check for the members added to the Household. The right side shows the Prime sharing benefits and more.

To add a Teen

Teens that a user or principal holder wants to add to the Amazon Household needs to have their own login which are connected to their parents account. Parents have the choice where to address delivery, approve orders placed by their teens, and share the credit card to be used for payment.

When a Teen places an order for an Amazon product, the parent will receive a message through text or email for every order placed by the teen notifying for the item ordered, its cost, address for delivery, and payment information. The parents can either approve the order through text or view the order from the order page to check the details of the transaction. The parent has the option to cancel the order or return the order in accordance with Amazon's policies.

The Teen whose parents are Prime members gets to share Prime shipping, Prime Video, and Twitch Prime. Parents, though, need not worry about what their Teens can view on these devices are they can manage and control viewing in **Manage Your Content and Devices**.

To add a child

- Go back to Manage Your Household and click **Add a Child**
- Enter the name of your child, birth date, and select an icon for your child's profile then **click Save**

Sharing Family Library Content

You can share the contents of the Family Library only to members of your Amazon Household. With the Family Library enables, you can share Kindle books, games, and apps. Included in what you can share under Family Library are books you borrowed from a public library and books on loan to your through personal lending. Shared books can be read on compatible e-readers.

How to share Family Library

- Navigate to **Manage Your Content and Devices,** select **Your Content**
- From the Your Content tab, select **Show** then chose the content you would like to share
- Check the box beside the content you would to share and select **Add to Library.** You can add as many books as you want simultaneously.
- If the Add to Library does not appear after checking a box, select **Show Family Library**

- Select a profile from the menu and click **OK.**

Managing sharing content with your child

Managing the sharing of content of the Family Library is where the power lies. Family Library allows you to control what your children can view in your Family Library and limit viewable contents to that which are age-appropriate. You would need a Kindle e-reader to view Kindle library content. Here are the steps on how to control sharing:

Note: Free Time is accessible on compatible phone, desktop, and tablet. Note that Family Library is by default turned off on all Kindle-reading apps. To enable shared Family Library on any of the listed devices above, install the device you want the content to share with. At present, Free Time is not supported by the Amazon Fire Stick. But, with the constant upgrade Amazon does on their devices, it will not be a surprise if Fire Stick is able to support FreeTime for children.

- Open Amazon Free Time on your device to view profiles added to the Amazon Household
- Open FreeTime on your Kindle e-reader and access profiles entered in Amazon Household
- Open your browser and navigate to **Manage Your Content and Devices**
- Sign in then click **YourDevices**
- Under Your Devices, click the device you want to share the content with
- Check the box beside **Show [adult/Teen/Child] Content**

PIN for secure purchases and viewing control

PIN is necessary for a user to prevent unauthorized purchases, prevent access to restricted areas, and to manage and control viewing privileges of Teens and children in your Amazon Household.

If you are new to Amazon services, you get a prompt to create a PIN as soon as you set up your device. If you are already a Prime member, the prompt will tell you to use existing PIN. The PIN which you may have obtained from a purchase of any Amazon device or streaming service can be used across all devices. You do have the option to change your PIN, should you want to. If you happen to forget what your PIN was, you can create another PIN by going to your Amazon account and go to the web-based control center.

Sharing Prime Benefits with the Amazon Household

Amazon Household allows members to share Prime Benefits for as long as the principal holder or the adults are Prime members. The adults in Amazon Household should have both their accounts linked and agree that payment methods be shared. Prime benefits are shared with no added costs to members of the Amazon Household..

The following benefits are shared:
- Free Prime shipping
- Prime Now
- Amazon Fresh
- Prime Video
- Prime Photos
- Audible Channels
- Kindle Owners' Lending Library
- Avail of discounts and unique benefits
    - Prime Early Access

- Exclusive pricing set by Prime on FreeTime Unlimited subscriptions and Amazon Music Unlimited

In addition, the following benefits are eligible for sharing but limited to age-appropriate conditions:

- Family Vault – Prime members are eligible to share photos contained in the Family Vault of up to five people but limited to those who are 13 years old and over
- Twitch Prime – this refers to the benefits provided by Amazon Prime for gamers. Existing membership to Amazon Prime and Prime Student gets the following benefits:

  - Share twitch benefits
  - Connect Twitch accounts to a maximum of four, have fun with ad-free viewing, and avail of the exclusive chat emoticons
  - Access to free games, including in-game loot
  - First user appearing in the list of shared account can avail of a free channel subscription

Conclusion

Providing you with a comprehensive picture of such a small but amazing device will help you navigate through the different streaming services and applications. As mentioned in the initial part of this book, what makes the Amazon Fire Stick a popular choice, especially among people on the go, is its portability, the services offered, and the various applications the device contains and those that you can add as a Fire Stick user.

To this end, the book presents and discusses its streaming services, to wit, Amazon Prime Video, Amazon Video, and Amazon Channels. It is hoped that after reading the chapters dealing with the three streaming services, you would have distinguished the distinct features of each and helped you decide which is appropriate for you. Though, should you wish to, you could become a member of two or all three to avail of the different services offered by each streaming technology.

Attention is also given to significant features of the different applications contained in the Amazon Fire Stick, such as the voice-controlled virtual personal assistant Alexa and its companion the Echo devices. Both will make your Fire Stick experience richer.

Setting up the different services and applications are provided in this book with the goal of making it fast and easy for you to complete the set up and move directly to making the most of our Fire Stick and start enjoying its contents. The next step is to act now and get an Amazon Fire Stick. Amazon constantly adds features, offers, and freebies on any of its applications and services. The sooner you get the device, the more you will have of these added features and offers.

I wish you the best of luck!

To your success,

William Seals

Made in the USA
Columbia, SC
14 November 2022